COVER **TO** BIBLE **STUDY**

CW00409652

David

A MAN AFTER GOD'S OWN HEART

CWR

Claire Musters

Contents

Introduction

The story of David is found in 1 and 2 Samuel. As children
we are taught about the great story of the young man
conquering the giant, when David faced and killed Goliath.
As we get older, we may then breathe a sigh of relief when
we read how David wasn't perfect, but acted impulsively
and sinfully in his relationship with Bathsheba. The depths
that he went to were so shocking that it must make us
glad that God doesn't write off anyone who truly repents.
Indeed, despite his shortcomings, God called David 'a man
after [my] own heart' (1 Sam. 13:14) so what was it about
his life and the way he lived it that caused God to say that?
What can we learn from him – from both his victories but
also his mistakes?

What is so fascinating about David's story is that we are
shown everything: his courage and generosity, his musical
talent (he has given us an amazing legacy in the large
amount of psalms he penned) and depth of honesty and
integrity, but also his human frailty and foolishness. Of
course, he is also part of Jesus' family line.

When we first meet David in the Bible, Saul is king.
In fact Saul has become the first king of Israel, selected
after the people grumbled and asked to have a king like
all the other nations (1 Sam. 8:6–9,19–20). Samuel was a
great prophet active throughout this time and he had the
privilege of anointing both Saul and David.

Saul began his kingship well. He was an obvious choice:
strong, striking yet humble, and God's Spirit was with him.
He listened to Samuel's counsel and was known for his
bravery (1 Sam. 14:46–48). But then he disobeyed God
(see chapters 13 and 15), he became jealous and paranoid
until eventually God removed His blessing and approval
from him.

God directed Samuel to David for the new king. At the time, David was not the obvious choice, but a hidden, faithful shepherd boy. We will look at how God raised him up to be a great king, using his humble beginnings as a training ground for great leadership. But that doesn't mean he immediately took the throne from Saul – or that he was without faults.

The Bible doesn't shy away from recording the worst as well as the best moments of David's life, and that is one of the things I love about his story. While we are shocked by some of his actions, such as committing adultery and basically instigating murder, it can be both sobering and challenging to consider how easily we can be swayed off course too.

As Christians living out our faith in the reality of our daily circumstances, we need to be honest about how we don't always live out our faith well. However, I think we can take great comfort from knowing that, even when David got things wrong, God didn't leave him. It is vital to note that David was quick to repent, and wasn't immune from the consequences of his actions, but God still cherished him.

What I believe God loved about David was the honesty and freedom with which he shared his heart and worshipped Him. He didn't allow the pressure of public office to affect his almost childlike delight in God, and certainly didn't bow to the opinion of others when he knew it would hinder his worship. How often do we allow others' opinions of us to curtail a full freedom of expression in our relationship with God?

There are many psalms written by David, within them we can see how he expressed his emotions freely – including his darkest ones. He also reminded himself to trust in God and lifted his eyes heavenward at every opportunity.

We can sometimes feel like we have to smother our negative feelings in order to come before God, and yet David's writing, particularly in the psalms, reveals to us how he struggled and trusted in tandem – his writing reminds us that dealing with difficult emotions and situations is a journey, a process. Psalm 55 is a great example. He begins by feeling fear: 'My heart is in anguish within me; the terrors of death have fallen on me' (v4). But trust is a choice; we need to step out in faith, remind ourselves who we really are in God and then the feelings will eventually follow, as we can see in verses 16–18 and 22, which say, 'Cast your cares on the LORD and he will sustain you'. We can mistakenly think we need to conquer what we are feeling before we can step out in faith, but often God asks us to step out first, despite our feelings.

I find that I come back to David's story time and time again. As a worship leader I can sometimes struggle to see above the difficulties in my life, but David teaches me so much about how to do that. I find that I often use his songs as a template for my own worship times and psalm writing too.

We can learn so much from this man of God; my prayer is that this study guide will start a journey of discovery for you. Why not take some time right now to open your heart to God and ask Him to reveal to you everything He wants you to learn from David's life?

WEEK 1

An Unseen Apprenticeship

Opening Icebreaker

Think about some of the things that you do 'behind the scenes' and discuss in pairs what you feel God could be teaching you through those activities.

Bible Readings

- 1 Samuel 16:1–13 (David anointed)
- 1 Samuel 16:14–23 (in Saul's service)
- Psalm 78:70–72
- Psalm 89:20–29

Opening Our Eyes

Just before our readings, in 1 Samuel 15 God clearly shows Saul that he is no longer fit to be king – God withdraws His blessing from him. At the start of the next chapter, Samuel is still coming to terms with this – God describes it as him 'mourn[ing] for Saul' (1 Sam. 16:1). He instructs Samuel to fill his horn with oil and go to Jesse as one of his sons is to be the next king.

Both Samuel and Jesse assume that God is going to pick one of the strongest-looking sons but God clearly states that His agenda is different to ours: 'The LORD does not look at the things people look at. People look at the outward appearance, but the LORD looks at the heart' (v7). How often do we judge by outward appearances only, especially when we first see someone? Psalm 89 shows us that God found David, his servant, and delighted to be with him.

It was the young son, who wasn't even in the room at the time, that God had appointed to lead His people. While Jesse may have disregarded him, God had remembered and chosen him. He saw qualities in David that others may have overlooked. It was the son who was out tending the sheep, faithfully serving his father and his livelihood, that was to be king. Isn't it interesting to note that it was during the years of preparation, when David was unknown and unseen while shepherding his father's sheep, that he was able to hone the skills he never knew he would need as a king, and yet were vital. God weaves our lives together like that too, so we need to learn not to despise the place where we are as we have no idea where God will take us in the future. Indeed, later in chapter 17 David reassures Saul that he has the skills to face Goliath because he has protected his family's sheep from lions and bears (vv34–37).

It is interesting to note that God didn't immediately hoist Saul from the throne and crown David king. Yes he was anointed, but it would be many years before he was able to rule as king. In fact, in the second half of chapter 16 we read that David has to learn to serve the very man he would replace! Here it is revealed that David has a sensitivity and gifting with music – so much so that he could calm Saul's troubled soul. Saul, of course, had no idea that he was calling on the services of the very man God had anointed to replace him but what a test it was for David's character. However, it also gave him a unique insight into the way Saul's kingdom was run as well as continuing his apprenticeship as a tenderer of sheep (1 Sam. 17:15 shows us he continued to do both activities).

Discussion Starters

1. Try to imagine you are in Samuel's shoes at the start of 1 Samuel 16. How would you feel about God asking you to go, in secret, and anoint someone else to be king while the king you have been serving is still on the throne?

_____

_____

_____

_____

2. God explains to Samuel that He looks at the heart. What sort of qualities do you think God is looking for? Why was David right for the job, while his brothers weren't?

_____

_____

_____

_____

3. Discuss what you know about the symbolism of being anointed with oil, as David was by Samuel.

_____

_____

_____

_____

4. How do you think David's brothers responded when Samuel hears from God that none of them were 'the one'; when they simply had to wait and then watch David be anointed, even though he was the youngest among them?

_____

_____

_____

_____

5. Spend some time individually, imagining how David must have felt when he was asked into the service of the king he had been anointed to replace. Share those emotions with each other.

_____

_____

_____

_____

6. What do you think the evil spirit that tormented Saul, which the Bible says came from 'the LORD' (v14), could have been?

_____

_____

_____

_____

7. Why do you think God orchestrated it so that it was David who was the only one that could relieve Saul's soul and get the evil spirit to stop tormenting him?

_____

_____

_____

_____

8. Think about the role music can have in soothing our emotions. Why do you think that is? How was music important in the lives of God's people?

_____

_____

_____

_____

Personal Application

Our society today can be very self-centred, self-sufficient and individualistic. The underlying message, perhaps, is that we should do all we can to push ourselves forward and get as far up the ladder as we can. David, however, was content to be faithful with where he had been placed and leaned wholeheartedly into God's strength rather than his own. His story shows us that often God has another way. Even when He gives us a foretaste of what it is He is calling us into, He often takes us on a roundabout way to continue working on our characters, getting us ready for what he has prepared for us. Reflect today on where God has placed you, and how you are dealing with any unfulfilled promises in your life. Do you need to say sorry for trying to rush ahead of God? Do you need to take some time to simply wait before Him?

Seeing Jesus in the Scriptures

David provides us with a great picture of our Saviour. Jesus came from the same line as David and, interestingly, He too was not the obvious choice of Saviour. The Jews were longing for a strong, warrior-like man who would defeat the Romans who were oppressing them. Instead, Scripture tells us that 'He had no beauty or majesty to attract us to him, nothing in his appearance that we should desire him' (Isa. 53:2). Yet again, God's chosen One had the right inner qualities but humans looked to the outer appearance and saw someone lowly. Jesus was born quietly, to a young girl in a stable. He grew up within a carpenter's family, content to learn His earthly father's craft. He waited patiently until His Father deemed it time for Him to start His ministry. Throughout this time He displayed the qualities of love, humility and gentleness that God so desires in us too.

WEEK 2

Facing the Giant

Opening Icebreaker

What is the one thing that feels like a giant in your life right now? Ask God for His perspective in order to face it with faith rather than fear. Share and pray with someone near you.

Bible Reading

- 1 Samuel 17 (facing Goliath)

Opening Our Eyes

We are focusing on this chapter this week as it is so pivotal to David's story. In this passage, we see that the Philistines have positioned themselves for war against the Israelites – in territory that rightly belonged to the people of God. Battles were sometimes decided through a fight between the best warriors on each side. This saved the armies the high cost of war in terms of human life and weaponry. It may seem strange that the stand off between both armies went on for forty days, but they were at either side of a valley, so whoever made a move down into it and up towards their enemy would have been at a distinct disadvantage.

When the Israelites were challenged by the Philistines' champion, each one of Saul's army, including himself (the obvious choice of opponent as the tallest Israelite), shrank back with fear. They looked at the giant before them and immediately concluded that they could do nothing and just waited glumly, expecting the worst. This reminds me of the Israelites when they were on the edge of the promised land but saw how big the inhabitants were (Num. 13:31–33).

At the point we are told that all of Israel are 'dismayed and terrified' (v11), we are reminded of David and where he comes from (the son of Jesse from Bethlehem and the youngest of eight boys). It is interesting that this information is repeated and we are also told that David obediently carries out his father's wishes to visit his brothers on the front line even though he has been anointed king. When David arrives he looks at the situation through the eyes of faith and immediately asks what the current king will do for the one who slays the giant. David doesn't see the giant as a threat; rather he sees Goliath as one who is defying God and is confident God will help him be defeated.

David's own brother mocks and criticises him (see vv26–30), but David's comments are heard and passed on to Saul. When he sees who it is, Saul says 'you are only a young man' (v33), looking at his outward appearance again. David, however, has confidence in who he is – and who his God is. He reveals the training that shepherding has given him (vv34–37) and persuades Saul to let him fight Goliath.

Interestingly, even though Saul is willing to place his trust in David, he still wants to dress him up to be like him. While some may have viewed being offered the armour of their king a huge privilege, David is honest and explains that he cannot walk freely and so cannot accept it. He chooses to use the simple tools that he used to kill lions and bears in the wild (v40).

Then comes the biggest test. The Philistine giant mocks and even curses him. But look how well David answers – he can see that he is little and insignificant in everyone else's eyes, but states that it will only serve to prove how great his God is when he has the victory. What an amazing comeback, which he follows through by using the skill he has learned to perfect. His little stone hits the spot exactly and he is able finish Goliath off with his own sword! The young shepherd becomes a giant slayer, and gives the whole nation the courage to see the rest of the Philistines off.

??? Discussion Starters

1. What was it that set David apart from all the others in Israel?

_____

_____

_____

_____

2. Why do you think this passage repeats the information about where David was from?

_____

_____

_____

_____

3. Discuss the specific things that caused the Israelites to shrink in their own eyes. Can you think of any situations that you have been in that have caused you to lose hope and see yourself as less than you truly are in God's eyes?

_____

_____

_____

_____

4. Now picture that same situation with you standing in the middle of it, surrounded by thousands upon thousands of angels, armed and ready to do battle on your behalf. What scriptures can you bring to mind that remind you that the 'battle is the LORD's' (1 Sam. 17:47) and that you can be on the offensive instead of the defensive in such situations?

_____

_____

_____

_____

5. Imagine what a leap of courage and faith it must have been for David to stand in front of Goliath armed just with his sling and small stones. Can you think of other instances in which God uses what seems like tiny resources to change big situations?

_____

_____

_____

_____

6. What was the Philistine and Israelite response to the death of Goliath?

_____

_____

_____

_____

7. What can those responses teach us about the role of faith not only in our own lives, but those around us too?

_____

_____

_____

_____

8. Interestingly, at the end of chapter 17 we read that Saul doesn't know who David is, even though David has regularly played the harp for him. Why do you think that is?

_____

_____

_____

_____

Personal Application

Fear and passivity can cause us to conform to the opinions, preferences and expectations of those around us. It can lead to situations like the one we find the Israelites in at the start of this chapter – all afraid, hiding from their enemy, no one with courage enough to stand up and out of the crowd. How wonderful, but also challenging, to read how David refused to be put in such a box by those around him (and even the king). How often do we stand up to opposition, even from those in our own friendship groups, in the same way that David did – or is our more usual response like that of the Israelites? David's perspective was very much in line with God's. David showed an almost childlike trust in God, but also in the training God had given him during his years as a shepherd. From which perspective are you seeing the challenges that lay before you?

Seeing Jesus in the Scriptures

The parallel that strikes me between David and Jesus from this passage is how they knew their authority in God and refused to be moulded and shaped into the expected image people had for the one they wanted as their champion. Rather than being a huge, burly Roman-slayer, Jesus came gently, but with a message that totally turned the Jews' preconceived ideas on their heads. We can, and should, view Jesus as our ultimate champion, as He has stood up to and defeated sin and death for good on our behalf. Our champion allowed Himself to be battered, bruised and crushed as He knew it was the only way to bring us life. How amazing – but how different from the way that we would probably envisage a champion to be.

WEEK 3

A Friend Who Sticks Closer Than a Brother

Opening Icebreaker

Think of a close friend. What is it about them that really uplifts and encourages you?

Bible Readings

- 1 Samuel 18:1–30 (the start of a deep friendship)
- 1 Samuel 19:1–24 (peacemaker and protector)
- 1 Samuel 20:1–42 (the covenant of friendship)
- Proverbs 18:24

Opening Our Eyes

It is at the start of chapter 18 that we are introduced to the person who will become David's closest friend. So many different events go on in these three chapters, but it is Jonathan who plays the pivotal supporting role.

It is so important for us to have friends who will help us to be all that we can be. As David was no longer going to be able to carry on his kingly apprenticeship in secret, God brought someone to him who would help him to continue to develop his character even in the midst of the public eye. Indeed, David would need to learn to deal with huge adulation from the people, poisonous jealousy and fear from the king and being married to the king's daughter.

The Bible tells us that as soon as Jonathan and David met, they 'became one in spirit' and each 'loved him as himself' (1 Sam. 18:1). Soon after, we read that Saul becomes increasingly jealous of the way David has captured the crowds. Saul decides to send David to battle, but, once he has more success, begins to hope David will be killed. Next he 'rewards' David with his daughter's hand in marriage, hoping that 'she may be a snare to him' (v20). In each of these steps, it appears that God is taking David through a process to refine his character. His response reveals that his heart is continuing to be purified, rather than tainted.

By remaining friends with David once his father was seeking to kill him, Jonathan's loyalties were split between his family and his friendship. And yet never once did he let David down – not even when he realised that it was David who was to be king, rather than him. He could have so easily been swayed against his friend when he realised his own position was no longer available. And yet he remains true: indeed, later, in chapter 23, when Jonathan voices out loud for the first time his recognition of God calling David to the throne, it is in the context of helping David 'to find strength in God' (vv16–17). That is a vital role of a friend: pointing not to themselves, but to God.

In chapter 19 we see Jonathan becoming the mediator. The peace is short-lived, however, and it is David's wife who helps him escape this time. When David flees he spends time with Samuel – the one person who he knows will continue to help mould him, rather than someone who will massage any sense of self-pity and injustice in his heart.

The friendship between Jonathan and David is so deep by the time that David flees that he doesn't think twice about approaching Jonathan, even though it could put them both in danger. He confides in him – although it is difficult for Jonathan to believe what is happening. Saul has recognised the depth of the bond between them and doesn't want Jonathan helping his enemy so keeps him in the dark.

Chapter 20 does not show David in his best light. He is now, somewhat understandably, focusing on his safety, and, taking matters into his own hands, asks his friend to tell a white lie to test out where things stand. Of course, this plan backfires and Saul becomes even angrier, lashing out at his son. This is to be the point at which the friends have to part, as David flees once again.

Discussion Starters

1. Why do you think the friendship between Jonathan and David is often described as one of the closest in the Bible? Think about some of the characteristics of their friendship, and what we can learn from them.

2. Why do you think deep friendships are important? Are there ways in which you can learn to be a Jonathan-like friend to someone in your life right now? Discuss this with the person next to you.

3. Brainstorm some of the scriptures that reveal to us that God wants each of us to love others like we love ourselves.

4. In what ways could the friendship between these two men have gotten in the way of the calling David had on his life?

5. Look at verses 13–15 in chapter 20 – what does this tell you about Jonathan?

_____

_____

_____

_____

6. In chapter 20 Jonathan agrees to cover for David – do you agree this was the best course of action or should he have done something different?

_____

_____

_____

_____

7. What do you think God is teaching David through the backfiring of the plan in chapter 20?

_____

_____

_____

_____

8. Why do you think scripture includes the detail 'they kissed each other and wept together – _but David wept the most_' (1 Sam. 20:41, emphasis mine)?

_____

_____

_____

_____

Personal Application

True friends watch out for one another, accept each other as they are but also have the guts to speak 'the truth in love' (Eph. 4:15). I have noticed that even those in churches can have a hard time accepting both love and discipline from friends around them. But we are called to reveal God's love through the way we love one another (John 13:34–35). Jonathan graciously stepped back from what was his right as heir to the throne, and dedicated his life to trying to keep his friend safe in order for him to fulfil God's calling on his life. How many of us can say we regularly champion our friends over ourselves? It is certainly humbling to read how Jonathan selflessly served his friend. God's plans were uppermost in his mind.

Seeing Jesus in the Scriptures

Time and time again Jonathan put himself in his father's firing line in order to protect his closest friend. Focusing on his friendship has reminded me that this was the very thing that Jesus came to do for us. He took His Father's just wrath upon Himself on the cross in order that the way could be opened up for us to be friends – adopted children even – of God. Jesus called His disciples to this selfless way of life too: 'My command is this: love each other as I have loved you. Greater love has no one than this: to lay down one's life for one's friends' (John 15:12–13). We are also told in Romans to always think of others above ourselves, 'Be devoted to one another in love. Honour one another above yourselves' (Rom 12:10). God commands us in this way because He knows that such depth of friendship is necessary in a world in which we face many adversities day by day. It is also the way in which God's love is revealed to the world too: 'No one has ever seen God; but if we love one another, God lives in us and his love is made complete in us' (1 John 4:12).

WEEK 4

Man on the Run

Opening Icebreaker

Hand round a few tubes of toothpaste and ask people to squeeze them and then discuss the different effects of putting pressure on something, both the positive and the negative.

Bible Readings

- Psalm 57
- 1 Samuel 23 (learning to listen to God again)
- Psalm 18
- 1 Samuel 24 (sparing Saul's life)
- 1 Samuel 26 (sparing Saul again)

Opening Our Eyes

In the previous two chapters David had taken some actions that were rooted in fear: he talked Ahimelech into giving him the consecrated bread, and also feigned madness in order to keep safe while at Gath (a Philistine city). The first action resulted, sadly, in Saul killing 85 priests (1 Sam. 22:9–19). Finally, in chapter 23, after the linen ephod had been brought to him, we see David asking God what he should do – both in regards to saving the city of Keilah and in discerning whether Saul is indeed pursuing him with the intent to kill him. In response to this, David and his men spend time in the desert, hills and caves – a far cry from the king's palace he must have expected to be living in by then!

What is interesting to note, however, is that David is going back to what he knows: how to listen to God's voice. He learnt that as a young shepherd for himself, but now he is learning to hear God for how to lead the people. By this point he had around 400 men gathered who were loyal to him. It wasn't about his own personal safety anymore: it was about learning to lead his men in a godly way – all great preparation for when he did become king.

As we have seen, David had a musical talent, and worshipping God was a huge part of that. From his experiences as a shepherd he had penned psalms such as Psalm 23, which celebrated his close personal relationship with God. He used music as a way of expressing himself to God. Indeed, even when he was feeling the weight of constantly having to be on his guard because he was being unjustly hounded, he wrote psalms that poured out his feelings of frustration. Psalms 18 and 57 are just two examples. But do note how, even in the midst of all the turmoil, he turned his attention to how great his God is. We can learn a lot about how to relate to God during the hard times from his psalms.

During his time on the run from Saul, it seems as if God gave David opportunities to redeem himself. He had taken matters into his own hands previously, but twice (in chapters 24 and 26) Saul comes right to him and he could easily have seized those moments to kill the king. However, as he says in 24:10, 'I will not lay my hand on my lord, because he is the LORD's anointed'. He recognises it is not his place to do so, and submits to God's lordship. Even though God had withdrawn His hand of blessing from Saul, David knew that it was up to Him to deal with Saul.

David puts himself in danger by speaking directly to Saul twice, giving him the chance to recognise the folly behind his constant pursuit. Both times Saul speaks of knowing that David is more righteous than he, and that God's hand is on him, and yet, while he lets David go, he changes his mind and chases after him again. David is shrewd enough to understand that the danger is not over and so stays where he is even when Saul invites him to go with him. This time on the run, when the pressure must have been getting to him, actually causes David to mature – both as a man and a leader.

Discussion Starters

1. What do you know about the significance of the linen ephod?

_____

_____

_____

_____

_____

2. What can you learn from David's psalms about facing difficult circumstances?

_____

_____

_____

_____

_____

3. Spend some time, either individually or as a group, writing a psalm that touches on some of the issues you struggle with but also highlights the greatness of God.

_____

_____

_____

_____

_____

4. What are some of the practical difficulties that you think David and his men would have experienced during their time on the run? What could this have tempted them to do?

_____

_____

_____

_____

_____

5. Why do you think Saul enters the cave by himself?

_____

_____

_____

_____

_____

6. Imagine you are David, tired out from the endless running. Picture either the scene in the cave, or when Saul is asleep in the camp. You have the opportunity to end the chase right then and there by killing the man pursuing you. How do you think you would respond?

_____

_____

_____

_____

_____

7. In chapter 26, why do you think David took the spear and water jug but spared Saul?

_____

_____

_____

_____

_____

8. What scriptures can you call to mind about how we are to treat those who seek to harm us?

_____

_____

_____

_____

_____

Personal Application

David was anointed to be king, and yet spent many years living on the run and hiding in caves. Difficulties in our lives refine, teach and prepare us for the things God has for us in the future (see Rom. 5:3–5). David risks his life when he calls out to Saul, but, in doing so, he is giving Saul the opportunity to repent. David doesn't retaliate against Saul, but recognises that there are others behind his actions, fuelling his fear and anger (see 24:9 and 26:19). David also continues to honour and respect him even though Saul is badly treating him. Is there someone in your life right now, perhaps a work colleague, family member or neighbour, who you feel is treating you unjustly? In the light of David's example, and the scriptures you have looked up, what do you think God is saying to you about them?

Seeing Jesus in the Scriptures

The time that David spent in the desert, wasteland and caves reminds me of Jesus' time in the wilderness. In Matthew 4, Jesus is led by the Spirit into the wilderness and is tempted by the devil. Jesus remains absolutely faithful and full of trust in His Father. Even though the devil tried every temptation and trick he could think of, Jesus did not sin. Like David, Jesus knew the importance of serving only God, rather than man: 'it is written: "Worship the Lord your God, and serve him only"' (v10). Another similarity between them is their patience. David spends a long time waiting – even before he is on the run. Jesus also waited to start His ministry. Even when His brothers urged Him to show the world who He was but He stayed put (John 7:6). He knew how to wait patiently until God's perfect timing was revealed.

WEEK 5

Leading Well

Opening Icebreaker

Think of a leader you admire and tell the person next to you why that is.

Bible Readings

- 2 Samuel 1 (mourning his king and friend)
- 2 Samuel 2:1–7 (becoming king of Judah)
- 2 Samuel 2:8–3:5 (fighting between the houses of Saul and David)
- 2 Samuel 5 (king of Israel)
- 2 Samuel 6–7 (doing things right before God)
- 2 Samuel 8 and 10 (David's victories)

Opening Our Eyes

The latter part of 1 Samuel reveals that David spent time living amongst the Philistines and Saul stopped pursuing him. David may have assumed that his own common sense had saved him – even though he had to lie to keep safe. He found favour with Achish and became his bodyguard. This put him in an awkward position as he ended up fighting alongside the Philistines against Israel. The prophet Samuel died during this time. Other Philistines decided they no longer wanted David among them so he was sent to Ziklag, where he discovered a raiding party had plundered it and taken wives and children captive, including his own two wives. By this point, he has repented of following his own plans so enquires of the Lord whether to pursue them; he successfully rescues everyone. Just before the end of 1 Samuel, the Philistines fight and kill Saul's sons, including Jonathan, and Saul takes his own life.

We begin our readings with David learning about Saul's death. The way is now open for him to become king, but he takes time to mourn and fast for both Saul and Jonathan. He pens a lament for them, which he teaches to the men of Judah.

He is in no rush to take the throne – 2:1 tells us time passes and he enquires of the Lord first. He becomes the king of Judah but Abner, commander of Saul's army, makes Saul's son Ish-bosheth king over Israel. What follows is a series of fights; as the house of Saul grows weaker, David's grows stronger. Even though some of his commanders take actions he does not know about, and later disapproves of, the way David deals with it all results in the people trusting his leadership. Indeed, 2 Samuel 3:36 says, 'all the people took note and were pleased; indeed, everything the king did pleased them'.

David's first actions as king show that God is uppermost in his mind: he takes back Jerusalem, defeats the Philistines and takes the ark to Jerusalem. David makes a big deal of the ark arriving: it is accompanied by huge celebrations. Even though he is now king, he is still totally at peace with submitting to the Lord as King over all, and dances and sings with all his might – much to his wife Michal's disgust (see chapter 6:16,20–23). He also sets up a tabernacle of worship on Mount Zion. As a shepherd boy he had hungered for God's people to worship God as they should and, as king, he was finally able to help facilitate that. However, God tells him he cannot build the Temple as he has spilled too much blood on the battlefield (see the details in 1 Chron. 22:6–10; 28:2–7, where the story is also told). Rather than complaining that he had been fighting on God's behalf, David submits to His decision readily.

David's actions please God and in chapter 7 we see God revealing to the prophet Nathan His promise that He will establish David's throne forever. David's response? He goes before the Lord in prayer, with humility and declarations of God's greatness.

The early years of David's reign are characterised by victories. He fights hard alongside his men and rules with justice and compassion (chapter 9 shows him taking Jonathan's crippled son to his table).

Discussion Starters

1. Take a look at David's lament. What does he focus on and how does he record Saul's life?

    _____

    _____

    _____

    _____

2. Can you think of any examples of when you (or someone you know) have begun to fulfil a role you feel God has called you to, only to face opposition? Why do you think that is?

    _____

    _____

    _____

    _____

3. Why was it important for David to be anointed for what was the third time when he became king of Israel?

    _____

    _____

    _____

    _____

4. What was the significance of the ark returning to Jerusalem? And why was Uzzah killed when he touched the ark, when he was trying to stop it falling off the cart?

    _____

    _____

    _____

    _____

5. Compare and contrast King David's and Michal's heart attitudes.

_____

_____

_____

_____

6. What do our passages this week reveal about David's priorities as king?

_____

_____

_____

_____

7. Can you remember a time when God spoke a promise over you? Also recollect some of the other promises God spoke over His people in the Bible. Spend some time reflecting on them and thanking God for the way He speaks promises into His people's lives.

_____

_____

_____

_____

8. What were some of the keys to David's success against his enemies?

_____

_____

_____

_____

Personal Application

As David finally takes the throne, we see he has developed into the kind of man God can use – fully dependent on Him, and more concerned about His glory rather than personal gain. We see David enquiring of the Lord before taking action. How often do we rush ahead with our own agenda, hoping God will come along and bless what we want to do rather than taking the time to ask Him what He wants us to do? The way David worshipped God wholeheartedly, even in the midst of going about his duties, is a great provocation too. Do you involve God in every aspect of your life? Do you consider how you display His glory through the actions you take daily or do you simply live in a reactive way to whatever life throws at you?

Seeing Jesus in the Scriptures

The way that God rescued His people through a humble man was a foretaste of what He would do through Jesus. David's first actions as king turned the people's attention back to God's promise of a Messiah. He felt the urgent need to recapture Jerusalem in order to remind the tribes of Israel that God *would* send them a Messiah. When David offers a sacrifice at his tabernacle on Mount Zion (6:17–18), he acts as priest and king, re-establishing the order of Melchizedek. When Melchizedek took the bread and wine to Abraham in Genesis 14, this was a foretaste of how Jesus would offer His body and blood for us outside the city walls. Interestingly, there was no Holy of Holies in this tabernacle. This is suggestive of the day when the Temple curtain would be torn in two in order for all to enjoy God's presence for themselves. This was something so much on David's heart: he longed for *all* the people to have the intimacy with God that he enjoyed.

WEEK 6

Idle Hands

Opening Icebreaker

There is a saying that dates back to at least Chaucer's time (the twelfth century): 'idle hands are the devil's workshop' (a more modern version of the phrase would be 'the devil finds work for idle hands'). Discuss the meaning of this saying, and whether people agree with it.

Bible Readings

- 2 Samuel 11 (falling into temptation)
- 2 Samuel 12:1–22 (confrontation and repentance)
- Psalm 51
- 2 Samuel 13 (the consequences of sin)

Opening Our Eyes

Even those who don't know much about the story of David are usually familiar with two episodes: him killing Goliath and his seduction of Bathsheba. It seems almost inconceivable that the man God chose as king because of his humble, upright heart, could stoop so low as to simply order a woman he liked to come to him, sleep with her and then try to cover it up. The lengths he went to do that were incredible, as he allowed Uriah to go to his death then took Bathsheba as his wife. But look how it all started: while his army is away fighting David stays home and is simply passing the time (11:1–2). He allows his gaze to go where it shouldn't – as soon as he lingers it quickly becomes a slippery slope that ends in him committing some huge sins. After each step he seems to become blinder to what he is doing. It seems that this was an area in which David was susceptible. Deuteronomy 17:17 states that a king 'must not take many wives, or his heart will be led astray'. David had already committed polygamy, collecting wives as they took his fancy and presumably not thinking too much of this disobedience while his actions seemed to go unpunished.

It is important to recognise that, however awful his actions seem to us, David accepted the consequences and repented quickly once challenged. Nathan was wise in the way he spoke to King David – telling a story that ended up with David condemning his own actions (see 12:1–6). David 'burned with anger' (v5) against the fictitious man – and owns up to his own sin and humbly accepts God's punishment soon after. We see him pouring out his repentance in Psalm 51, which he wrote at this time. He recognises that his sin was directed towards God, and asks Him to 'create in me a pure heart, O God, and renew a steadfast spirit within me' (Psa. 51:10). He also turns back to fasting and prayer, humbly pleading for his son's life.

When the boy dies, David continues to worship God for His goodness. We are told that he and Bathsheba have another son, Solomon. He would be the one who would build the Temple David had longed to build. So even after David displeased the Lord, He still kept His covenantal promise. David then goes back to the life he should have been leading at the head of his army (albeit after the slightly threatening message from Joab – see 12:28).

After some time has passed, we begin to see what the prophet Nathan had foretold happening. One of David's sons, Amnon, burns with lust for his sister. Egged on by a suggestion from his cousin Jonadab, he plots a way to get Tamar into his room (using his father in this process) and, once she is there, he rapes her. He then sends her away in shame. Her other brother, Absalom, dissuades her from making the matter public, but we later find out that he was simply biding his time in order to take out his revenge himself – through murdering his brother. How David must have been torn apart by the havoc that had been set loose inside his own family; tormented by the knowledge that he had set it off through his own deception and sin.

Discussion Starters

1. When you read about this episode in David's life, what is your initial response – outrage and judgement, or 'there but for the grace of God go I'?

2. Discuss the roles that others played in David's sin – such as Bathsheba and Joab. Do you think they shared some of the responsibility, or was it all down to the king?

3. Why was the prophet Nathan such a trustworthy companion to David?

4. How do people feel about being challenged by others about their behaviour? Is accountability encouraged in your church, or does it make you feel uncomfortable?

5. God doesn't allow sin to go unpunished, so why do you think He allowed David to remain on the throne after such awful deception and sin?

_____

_____

_____

_____

_____

6. Why was sending Tamar away adding to Amnon's crime?

_____

_____

_____

_____

_____

7. Why do you think David didn't punish Amnon?

_____

_____

_____

_____

_____

8. What is your understanding of the verses in Numbers that talk about the sins of the father being visited on the children: 'he does not leave the guilty unpunished; he punishes the children for the sin of the parents to the third and fourth generation' (Num. 14:18)? Do you think that this is what was happening in David's family?

_____

_____

_____

_____

_____

Personal Application

I draw comfort and hope from knowing that even the man whom God says was after his own heart was not perfect, and that God forgave him when he repented. However, there is a stark warning in David's story. We may feel that we would never sin in the huge way that David had, but just reflect again on the fact that a simple step led to more and more sin, and a dulling of his senses, until he didn't think twice about sending a man to his death and taking that man's wife as his own. How often can we make choices that make us more susceptible to sin? Choices that dull our senses and cause our hearts to entertain ideas and thoughts that block us from God's presence? David could have chosen to stop his actions at any point, but, as we see in his example, if we don't nip sin in the bud it gets harder to step away from it, as our hearts get more deeply entwined. David had to live with some heartbreaking consequences of his sin – God didn't let him or his family off the hook because he was a favourite. Let us soberly learn from this desperately sad episode in David's life.

Seeing Jesus in the Scriptures

Even though David was unfaithful in his actions, God remained faithful to him and continued the line of David that He said He would establish. It was this that paved the way for Jesus to be born into the Davidic family. God will remain faithful to us, even when we fail. We have this promise in 1 John 1:9: 'If we confess our sins, he is faithful and just and will forgive us our sins and purify us from all unrighteousness.' Our Saviour came to a world in dire need of Him – this particular episode reminds us that it was the only way God could save us.

WEEK 7

Growing Old

Opening Icebreaker

Try and put yourself in the position of David as an elderly king. What advice would you give to your younger self?

Bible Readings

- 2 Samuel 15; 16:15–22 (overthrown by his son)
- Psalm 63
- 2 Samuel 18–19 (mourning his son and returning to Israel)
- 2 Samuel 21–23:7 (re-establishing order; focusing on God)
- 1 Kings 1–2:12 (a last attempt for the throne; David's advice to Solomon)

Opening Our Eyes

While Absalom returned to David and it looked like there was peace in the family again, it wasn't long before Absalom was plotting. Look at 15:7 – he uses the guise of a vow he made to trick his father into letting him go to Hebron, which was his home town (see 3:2). From there, he gathered allegiances from right across Israel in order to take the crown for himself. David is grieved by his son's actions, but it was his inaction and lack of discipline that allowed this situation to occur. He does have the foresight to flee Jerusalem, and unnecessary bloodshed. Like he did with Saul's threat, he retreats and puts it all in God's hands.

Absalom's sin is reminiscent of both Saul's (power hungry) and David's (lustful) sins – but it is even more abhorrent. He lies with his father's concubines in full view, thus fulfilling the prophecy Nathan gave in 2 Samuel 12:11–12. In chapter 18, we see David move more decisively – where he had been indecisive he had given room for his son to look towards the throne but at last he musters his troops. Absalom is incapacitated, hanging in a tree, but David had asked his men not to kill him. It is Joab who takes it upon himself to kill Absalom. David mourns him deeply; so much so that the whole army felt it was a day of sadness instead of victory. It takes Joab speaking plainly to the king for him to return to Jerusalem (see 19:5–8).

While much of Israel had turned their backs on David to follow Absalom, they quickly turn back to him – chapter 19 details how David dealt with the various people as they came back with great wisdom and mercy. There follows a time of skirmishes between people who choose to rebel, and natural disasters such as famine to deal with. All these difficulties turn David back to enquiring of God (see 21:1) and his actions follow what God tells him to do.

The last chapters of 2 Samuel are not a chronological record; simply things that happened in David's life. In chapter 22 we see another song of David's, extremely similar to Psalm 18, in which he praises God for His great faithfulness. His last words are recorded in chapter 23, but we get a little more detail about the end of his life in 1 Kings. Another one of his sons, albeit the one most naturally assumed to take the throne on his father's death, sets himself up as king. 1 Kings 1:6 gives us an important detail – yet again, David had assumed his children would follow after both him and God, but he hadn't disciplined or taught them how to do so.

This time it is Nathan and Bathsheba who take matters into their own hands – by reminding the king of his oath of putting Solomon on the throne after him. While there isn't a direct reference to this when it happened, 1 Kings 1:17,30 show that Solomon was David's choice – and 1 Chronicles 22:9–10 reveals he was God's choice too. In 1 Kings 2 David speaks to Solomon, giving him advice on how to live and lead well, reminding him of what God requires. So, before he died, David had come full circle back to the desperate longing of knowing God more intimately (he wrote Psalm 63 while on the run from Absalom) and encouraging those who went after him to seek Him too.

Discussion Starters

1. Discuss some of the negative traits we can see in Absalom.

_____

_____

_____

_____

_____

2. Why do you think David mourns his son so deeply, even after he had usurped him and tried to take his throne?

_____

_____

_____

_____

_____

3. Think about the fickleness of the people of Israel and Judah. They turn from David so quickly, then turn back. What does this teach us about leadership and following the crowd's whims?

_____

_____

_____

_____

_____

4. Why do you think David gives those who rise against him the opportunity to repent?

_____

_____

_____

_____

_____

5. What does David's story teach us about our lives at home – including parenting?

_____
_____
_____
_____
_____

6. Why do you think David asked Solomon to kill some of the enemies he himself had promised not to harm?

_____
_____
_____
_____
_____

7. Remind yourselves of the qualities that David showed in his life that pleased God and which we know He longs for in us too.

_____
_____
_____
_____
_____

8. Share with one another the one thing that has struck you most in this exploration of the life of David – and how it has impacted you.

_____
_____
_____
_____
_____

Personal Application

Have you learned to call out to God for help, especially to keep you faithful to Him, as David did so often? We have a huge array of his psalms to help us understand how to do this. Have you also taught those under your care (whether your own children or people you guide and nurture spiritually) how to do the same? It is so important that we lead by example, but also help nourish the faith of those we have influence over. What sort of legacy do you hope to leave behind you that will impact the generations to come?

Seeing Jesus in the Scriptures

The rejection that David felt when his son was trying to take the throne is a picture of the way the city would reject Jesus. He follows the route that Jesus would on His way to be crucified. In his commentary on 1 and 2 Samuel, Phil Moore suggests that David's return to the city is a foretaste of Jesus' resurrection, because in chapter 17 he was as good as dead, but through friends he is given the chance to be restored.* He comes back as a king full of grace.

The fairness and generosity with which David dealt with those who had sided with his son set a standard for rule that will only be fully realised in the coming of Jesus' kingdom. It also gives us a taste of the welcome that God gives us when we choose to come to Him.

David's last words included a reference to the Messiah (2 Sam. 23:2–4), as he recognised there was a perfect ruler to come after him. Indeed, in 2 Samuel 24:17, David exclaims, 'These are but sheep. What have they done? Let your hand fall on me and my family', which is exactly what happened when Jesus took God's wrath in our place.

---

*Phil Moore, *Straight to the Heart of 1 & 2 Samuel* (Oxford: Monarch Books, 2012), p243.

Leader's Notes

These leader's notes have been written to support you as you lead your small group through what I hope will be informative and life-giving discussions together.

The Bible readings taken from 1 and 2 Samuel and 1 Kings have been briefly summarised in the Bible Readings section of each week so that you can see which part of David's life that week's readings will be covering. The psalms, while often written by David and with a connection to events in his life, are more poetic in form and of a timeless quality. These, along with the verse from Proverbs, are provided as supplementary readings to be read alongside David's life story.

Week 1: An Unseen Apprenticeship

Opening Icebreaker

This is aimed at getting people to think, right at the start, about their own lives, and how God may be working things through and training them for a future purpose.

Discussion Starters

1. Try to get people to think about how difficult it was for Samuel to go behind Saul's back to look for God's next anointed one. He had served Saul faithfully for years and, as we can see when he picks out the son he thinks God will choose, naturally felt that Saul's replacement would be like him.

2. Get the group thinking about how God wants us to be humble, teachable, faithful, not self-serving but pure and honest. While David's brothers may have looked impressive on the outside, it was only David, through his menial job as a shepherd, who had had his heart purified. His brothers had not faced the trials he had, and, as Phil Moore states, 'They could gladly serve in Saul's army because they grasped God's character as little as he did and shared his fear when the Philistine giant Goliath blasphemed the Lord's name by his pagan gods.'[1] Our reading from Psalm 78 shows how David tenderly, skillfully and with integrity looked after his father's sheep – those were qualities he nurtured behind the scenes, ready to take with him into kingship.

3. Anointing oil stood for holiness – it was a sign that David was now set apart. Such oil was used to indicate that someone (or something) had been set apart for God's service. Each king and priest

was anointed with oil in this way. We are told in
1 Samuel 16:13 that from the day that David was
anointed the Spirit of the Lord was upon him. Being
filled with the Holy Spirit was such a vital part of him
becoming the man God had chosen to lead.

4. There are both positive and negative emotions that
David's brothers may have felt – this is an interesting
exercise to see how people resonate with the passed-
over brothers. They may have been angry, jealous,
resentful – or they may have been proud of David,
recognising the pure qualities within him that God
saw. Knowing someone from their family would
be on the throne may have excited them, although
the more negative emotions could have had a more
immediate effect.

5. Try to get the group to think about how difficult
it must have been, but also what it taught David
about patience and waiting well. Was he frustrated?
Annoyed that God was asking him to serve the one
he knew was no longer deemed fit to be king? Or
was he cheerful, humble and glad of the opportunity
to learn more about the world he would eventually
enter as leader?

Having to wait would have taught him more about
how to make the most of the time, and it would have
continued to develop humility within him. We have
been told that the Holy Spirit came on David as he
was anointed (1 Sam. 16:13) and it was the Spirit
within him that allowed him to be content with simply
serving his father and current king, even though he
had the right to the crown.

6. It is interesting to note that it is when the Spirit of the Lord left Saul that an evil spirit then torments him. Some commentators say this could have simply been depression as a result of being rejected from kingship by God. Others say that God allowed a demon to torment him, thus showing God's power over the spirit world (see 1 Kings 22:19–23 for an example of this).

7. I think this provided David with an important lesson in still honouring and serving Saul until God removed him from the throne. Learning it at this point, as we shall see, helped him not to take matters into his own hands later.

8. Music has always been important to the lives of God's people – for example, among the Levites' daily duties was worshipping God with music. They also went ahead of the army in battles, sounding their trumpets. But what about its role in soothing emotions? Music has been used for centuries to improve moods and even speed up the healing process. In the 1990s new brain mapping techniques allowed scientists to see just how many areas of the brain music affects.

Here is a quote from the site: www.psychologicalscience.org[2]

'Researchers have shown that music stimulates the cerebellum, a region of the brain crucial to motor control. Levitin [psychological scientist] says connections between the cerebellum and the limbic system (which is associated with emotion), "may explain why movement, emotion, and music are tied together."'

[1]Phil Moore, *Straight to the Heart of 1 & 2 Samuel* (Oxford: Monarch Books, 2012), p94.
[2]http://www.psychologicalscience.org/index.php/publications/observer/obsonline/why-does-music-move-us.html

Week 2: Facing the Giant

Opening Icebreaker

So often we read this story and don't apply the principles to our own lives. This icebreaker encourages people to view the challenges they are facing right now from a different perspective – one of faith.

Discussion Starters

1. David saw the situation from God's perspective, not man's, and had the courage to speak words of faith and act on them. He was himself too – Saul tried to put his own armour on him but he couldn't walk in it so refused what could have been seen as man's protection and relied on what he had learned with God out in the fields.

2. It underlines the fact that God 'chose the foolish things of the world to shame the wise' (1 Cor. 1:27). David wasn't from an important family in Israel, and was even the youngest son, and yet he became the one to rescue the whole nation.

3. The Israelites were facing a huge army; the Philistine champion was over nine feet tall – he looked unbeatable; the Israelite king was cowering and hiding so they had no strong leader; they were positioned on one side of a valley so they really had nowhere to go. Try to share a story of your own, if necessary, to get a wider discussion going.

4. Here are some scriptures that you can look up and discuss: Deuteronomy 23:14; 2 Chronicles 16:9; 20:15; Isaiah 40:28–31; Isaiah 54:17; Psalm 18:32; 91; 144:1; Romans 8:31–37; 2 Timothy 4:18.

5. Here are a few examples to help kickstart the discussion as necessary: the feeding of the five thousand, Moses' staff on the ground to part the Red Sea and also bring forth water in the desert, Joseph rising from being a prisoner to vizier (second only to pharaoh) to help lead a whole nation through a time of famine.

6. As soon as the Philistines saw that their big hero was dead, they were gripped by fear (presumably wondering what god was behind this young man as he was able to defeat Goliath so easily). The Israelites responded positively, their spirits raised and faith buoyed by what had happened, and they kicked into action, killing Philistines as they retreated.

7. When one person steps out in faith and God moves, it creates an increased expectancy in those around them too. So while trusting in God does us, and our courage, good, it also helps spur on those around us – something God has commanded us to do 'spur one another on towards love and good deeds' (Heb. 10:24).

8. When Saul was being oppressed by the evil spirit, his mind would have been focused on his problem (in fact he may not even have been in his right mind). He was soothed by David's playing, but probably paid little attention to who he was (even though he had sent word to his father that he wanted him in his service) – just demanded that he be made available for when Saul needed him. A good leader finds out about those who serve them; by this point Saul was only interested in himself.

Week 3: A Friend Who Sticks Closer Than a Brother

Opening Icebreaker

This exercise is simply to get the group thinking about the characteristics that make a good friend, before they begin to read about Jonathan.

Discussion Starters

1. Their friendship was entwined with God – they were first and foremost committed to Him. They didn't let anything come between them, even when family pressures were huge. Jonathan, in particular, put his friend's needs before his own. They both remained faithful to their friendship throughout their lives. They didn't allow pressure to tear them apart, but worked hard to maintain their friendship.

2. Facilitate some open discussion between pairs in the group. It is interesting to note that Jonathan played a vital supporting role throughout his friendship with David, often risking his life to do so. We are not always called to be the leader – but can help make another person great if we faithfully serve them well.

3. Loving one another: Matthew 22:37–39, John 13:34–35, 15:12–13, Romans 12:10 and 1 John 4:7–21 are just a few examples.

4. As David got closer to Jonathan, the natural heir of the current king, he could have begun to forget the prophecy and anointing that had been made over him. He could have decided not to do anything that would put his friend in danger, and therefore stroke Saul's ego rather than rock the boat. Other things that

could have tempted David to act like this were being given a high rank in Saul's army and being married into Saul's family.

5. Jonathan recognised that God had chosen David to be the next king – he accepted it rather than fighting it, and helped his friend in any way he could so that he remained safe. What selflessness.

6. By telling a lie to his father, Jonathan is sinning. He is talked into it by David – whose fear is driving him at this point – and through an admirable desire to protect his friend. Try to get the group to come up with alternative courses of action that would mean Jonathan could remain a man of integrity.

7. God is teaching David that nothing but absolute integrity and trust in Him will work. He mustn't take matters into his own hands but wait patiently, as he had been doing up till now, and let the Lord act in His time.

8. David recognises that he must now part company with Jonathan, but in that moment probably felt a rush of emotion because of how much he cherished the role Jonathan had played in his life up until that point. The faithfulness of his friend had helped him through so many difficulties – but he is going to have to face many more dangers without him. He may well have been feeling overwhelmed by that. Jonathan would be returning to the comfort of the palace, but David would have to continue living on the run.

Week 4: Man on the Run

Opening Icebreaker

The toothpaste is an analogy of us. It is only when we are under pressure, being 'squeezed', that what is truly inside is revealed. Ask people to think about how they respond to pressure.

Discussion Starters

1. The ephod was a sleeveless linen vest worn by priests. It may have been the last symbol of priesthood that survived Saul's annihilation of the priests. While Saul had turned away from consulting God, David installs Abiathar as his priest (he remains priest throughout David's reign) and consults God about what actions he should take.

2. David was not afraid to pour out his emotions to God, including his despair. However, he was also quick to turn his attention to God's sovereignty and power – determined to sing of God's goodness in the midst of difficulties.

3. Try to encourage each person to participate in this. You could then share the psalms as a group, using them as prayers, or encourage people to use the psalm they have written (or write another one) in their own devotional times in the week.

4. David had 400 men with him – just gathering enough food, water and shelter for them all would have been a huge undertaking (indeed, while space has unfortunately not allowed me to focus on her story, Abigail plays a pivotal role in stopping David from

killing a host of men when her husband refused to provide for them). There would no doubt have been sicknesses that occurred too, and the temptation must have been to give up and surrender to Saul. When they had him within their reach, each one of them must have been tempted to kill Saul in order to end their ordeal.

5. Saul had had some success, had a larger army than David and was no doubt feeling puffed up and proud. He didn't even allow his bodyguard into the cave – perhaps because he didn't want anyone he led to see him relieve himself. He was probably feeling a sense of his own importance and seemed almost invincible to himself at this point.

6. Facilitate some open discussion, first answering how you would have responded, if necessary.

Try to ensure that the discussion brings out the point that even though he could be justified for doing so, and David's men were urging him to (using the very persuasive line 'God has given your enemy into your hand'), David stood resolutely to what he knew was right, looking to God for his next move rather than relying on man's reasoning.

7. David could have killed Saul, but chose not to. By taking the items he was showing that, but also proving that he had more respect for God and his anointed one. Even though God had said he was no longer with Saul, David recognised it was not his place to end Saul's life.

8. Here are some examples in case you need to start people off: Matthew 5:43–48; Luke 21:12–19; Ephesians 6:12; 1 Peter 2:12.

Week 5: Leading Well

Opening Icebreaker

This question is to get the group thinking about the admirable qualities of leaders they are happy to follow, as, once David was king, the people quickly followed him.

Discussion Starters

1. David focuses on the name of the Lord, grieving for what Saul and Jonathan's deaths will mean for Israel and how the Philistines must be celebrating that their gods have won. He graciously doesn't include Saul's faults but celebrates and mourns both his and Jonathan's lives.

2. Encourage discussion. Some of the reasons for opposition include jealousy, a lack of understanding of God's will, the enemy trying to trip you up before you really get going, etc. Often we have to fight to take the ground we believe God has told us to walk into.

3. While it wasn't strictly necessary, David being anointed for a third time was a turning point for Israel. The people recognised the victories David had had under Saul and what the prophet Samuel had spoken about him. They repented and all 12 tribes of Israel were finally united under one king.

4. The ark had been captured and held by Israel's enemies for too many years. As a symbol of God's presence, glory and power it was important to David that it was brought back. However, the parallel story in Chronicles reveals that he may have done what he thought was right in the eyes of the people rather than checking with

God (see 1 Chron. 13:1 – he confers with all his officers and commanders but we are not told he prays). David was confused and angry that God had struck Uzzah but he had forgotten that there were strict instructions about how the ark must be transported – wrapped up in the Tabernacle curtains and carried on poles by specific Levites (Exod. 25:12–15; Num. 4:5–12,15; 7:9). David had it on a cart! The first time it doesn't make it to Jerusalem – David gets scared when he sees what happens to Uzzah so leaves the ark at a nearby home. When he hears how it has caused blessing on that household, he returns to take it to Jerusalem, but this time follows God's instructions (see 1 Chron. 15).

5. Michal was looking to outward appearances, seeing David dancing in his ephod as 'beneath him', whereas David only had eyes for God, and wanted to please Him by offering wholehearted worship. Michal seemed focused on earthly position and what befitted a king, whereas David continued to humbly serve God.

6. David's priorities as king included reclaiming Jerusalem (it was the city of the people of God, and yet their enemies had repeatedly captured it), bringing the ark of the Covenant back, teaching the people to honour and hunger for God's presence (shown through his worship and his plans for the building of the Temple), honouring the Covenant and proclaiming the greatness of God to the nations.

7. Here are some of God's promises to the Israelites before the reign of David: to Abraham and his descendants God promised to make his descendants as numerous as the stars in the sky: Genesis 22:17–18. When God delivered the Israelites from the Egyptians He gave them a promise that they would be His treasured possession, the place He would dwell:

Exodus 19:5–6; Leviticus 26:11–13. Another promise to the Israelites, which is so precious to us today too: 'If ... you seek the LORD your God, you will find him if you seek him with all your heart and with all your soul' (Deut. 4:29). Joshua 21:43–45 talks of all God's promises to the Israelites being fulfilled.

8. Some of the keys to David's success include: listening to God for His direction, great strength and courage, encouraging his army to look to the Lord and fight for Him (2 Sam. 10:12) and acting with justice. He made it a priority to capture the *whole* of the promised land for God, at last.

Week 6: Idle Hands

Opening Icebreaker

This is to get people thinking about the fact that when we are not focused on what we are called to do, we can quickly be drawn into unhealthy thoughts and actions.

Discussion Starters

1. Try to analyse the group's responses – ask them why they think they respond as they do.

2. Bathsheba was put in an awkward position when David sent for her. She knew it was wrong to commit adultery but she could have been put to death for refusing her king's command. Joab didn't know why David wanted Uriah to be put to death, but he still complied with his orders. When both options seem wrong, we need to seek God for other ways forward.

3. Nathan was a true friend in that he heard God speak directly and wasn't afraid to confront the king. However, he was also wise and careful in the way that he spoke to David.

4. Try to facilitate an open discussion, encouraging people to feel that no answer is wrong so they are safe to speak up.

5. David sinned greatly, but he recognised his sin once it was pointed out to him and repented eagerly and wholeheartedly. He didn't try to talk his way out of it by pleading his self-righteousness, and also humbly accepted the consequences of his actions.

6. Rape was strictly forbidden (see Deut. 22:28). By sending Tamar away, Amnon was making it look like she had propositioned him. With no witnesses to say to the contrary (because Amnon had dismissed them all), there was no-one to stick up for Tamar and tell the truth. So Amnon had heaped double shame upon her, completely destroying her chances of marriage.

7. Perhaps he didn't punish Amnon because he was his firstborn and therefore heir to the throne, so he didn't want to get on the wrong side of him. But his own sin and guilt of an act of adultery may have stopped him too. David shows himself lacking in the area of sensitive and wise parenting.

8. God has given each one of us free will and we do make our own personal choices. However, it is clear to see how David's sin opened the way for similar sin to be committed by his sons. Amnon, for example, was acting out of lust – something that he would have known his father did. As soon as he had raped Tamar we are told he hated her.

Week 7: Growing Old

Opening Icebreaker

Give people time to think about and write down some advice. Then encourage (but don't force) each person to share one thing.

Discussion Starters

1. You could get people to look at 2 Samuel 14:25–33 to help with this. Absalom was proud, disobedient, unrepentant, harsh, impure, not concerned with being in line with God's words.

2. He probably understood his part in his son's death – the fact that Nathan had told him his own sons would rebel against him because he had killed Uriah. He would have been particularly upset that it was Joab who had killed him, when he had given direct orders for him not to. He also still loved his son deeply – even though he had not had the wisdom to show that love through discipline when Absalom was younger.

3. While it can be tempting to follow the opinion of the masses, people are generally fickle. Leaders must stick to following God rather than trying to please people, and use the Bible as a plumbline – not people's opinion.

4. He knew that God's heart was for people to turn back to him. That's why he had asked his officers to spare Absalom. He also gave Joab time to repent of his killing of Absalom and didn't force himself back onto Israel – he gave the people time to come to him. He was giving everyone the chance to repent, thus revealing God's heart for the sinner, which he himself had experienced.

5. David's story teaches us that however fine a leader or worker we may be out in the public eye, if our house is not in order someone from within it may well be our downfall. Our priority has to be loving and leading those within our household well. We cannot assume that our children will follow in our footsteps regarding their faith, if we haven't shown them how to.

6. While David had shown mercy, he was helping his son to establish his throne securely. His harsh advice was directed at those who were enemies. He was legally entitled to give them the punishment they deserved – for example, Shimei had cursed David back in 2 Samuel 16, and that was against civil and God's laws (see Exod. 22:28).

7. David was humble, honest, just, fair, passionate for God and worshipping Him, obedient and pure. However, there were times in his life when he was far from these things. What stood him out, though, was his quick repentance. We are not perfect, but God canuse a malleable, repentant heart.

8. Give the group time for reflection, but encourage each person to think of one thing that they will take away from this study to apply to their own life.

Notes …

Continue transforming your daily walk with God.

Every Day with Jesus

With around half a million readers, this insightful devotional by Selwyn Hughes is one of the most popular daily Bible reading tools in the world. A large-print edition is also available.
72-page booklets, 120x170mm

Life Every Day

Apply the Bible to life each day with these challenging life-application notes written by international speaker and well-known author Jeff Lucas.
64-page booklets, 120x170mm

Inspiring Women Every Day

Written by women for women of all ages and from all walks of life. These notes will help to build faith and bring encouragement and inspiration to the lives and hearts of Christian women.
64-page booklets, 120x170mm

Cover to Cover Every Day

Study one Old Testament and one New Testament book in depth with each issue, and a psalm every weekend. Covers every book of the Bible in five years.
64-page booklets, 120x170mm

Cover to Cover Every Day is now only available as an email subscription or eBook

For current prices or to order, visit **www.cwr.org.uk/store**
Available online or from Christian bookshops.

Journey through the Bible as it happened in a year of daily readings

Read through the entire Bible in a year with 366 daily readings from the New International Version (NIV) arranged in chronological order.

Beautiful charts, maps, illustrations and diagrams make the biblical background vivid, timelines enable you to track your progress, and a daily commentary helps you to apply what you read to your life.

A special website also provides character studies, insightful articles, photos of archaeological sites and much more for increased understanding and insight.

Cover to Cover Complete – NIV Edition
1,600 pages, hardback with ribbon marker, 140x215mm
ISBN: 978-1-85345-804-0

Latest resource

Thessalonians - Building Church in changing times

Paul's letters to the Thessalonians are addressed to a people needing guidance, a reminder of their core beliefs and encouragement to move from mere religion into a relationship with their Saviour - Jesus Christ. The same could be written to us today. Find out how God builds His Church, from the first Christians in ancient Thessalonica to His modern worldwide Church.

72-page booklet, 210x148mm
ISBN: 978-1-78259-443-7

The bestselling *Cover to Cover* Bible Study Series

1 Corinthians
Growing a Spirit-filled church
ISBN: 978-1-85345-374-8

2 Corinthians
Restoring harmony
ISBN: 978-1-85345-551-3

1 Peter
Good reasons for hope
ISBN: 978-1-78259-088-0

2 Peter
Living in the light of God's promises
ISBN: 978-1-78259-403-1

1 Timothy
Healthy churches –
effective Christians
ISBN: 978-1-85345-291-8

23rd Psalm
The Lord is my shepherd
ISBN: 978-1-85345-449-3

2 Timothy and Titus
Vital Christianity
ISBN: 978-1-85345-338-0

Abraham
Adventures of faith
ISBN: 978-1-78259-089-7

Acts 1–12
Church on the move
ISBN: 978-1-85345-574-2

Acts 13–28
To the ends of the earth
ISBN: 978-1-85345-592-6

Barnabas
Son of encouragement
ISBN: 978-1-85345-911-5

Bible Genres
Hearing what the Bible really says
ISBN: 978-1-85345-987-0

Daniel
Living boldly for God
ISBN: 978-1-85345-986-3

David
A man after God's own heart
ISBN: 978-1-78259-444-4

Ecclesiastes
Hard questions and
spiritual answers
ISBN: 978-1-85345-371-7

Elijah
A man and his God
ISBN: 978-1-85345-575-9

Ephesians
Claiming your inheritance
ISBN: 978-1-85345-229-1

Esther
For such a time as this
ISBN: 978-1-85345-511-7

Fruit of the Spirit
Growing more like Jesus
ISBN: 978-1-85345-375-5

Galatians
Freedom in Christ
ISBN: 978-1-85345-648-0

God's Rescue Plan
Finding God's fingerprints
on human history
ISBN: 978-1-85345-294-9

Great Prayers of the Bible
Applying them to our lives to
ISBN: 978-1-85345-253-6

Hebrews
Jesus – simply the best
ISBN: 978-1-85345-337-3

Hosea
The love that never fails
ISBN: 978-1-85345-290-1

smallGroup central

All of our small group ideas and resources in one place

Online:

www.smallgroupcentral.org.uk
is filled with free video teaching,
tools, articles and a whole host
of ideas.

On the road:

A range of seminars themed for
small groups can be brought to
your local community. Contact us at
hello@smallgroupcentral.org.uk

In print:

Books, study guides and DVDs
covering an extensive list of themes,
Bible books and life issues.

Log on and find out more at:
www.smallgroupcentral.org.uk

Courses and events

Waverley Abbey College

Publishing and media

Conference facilities

Transforming lives

CWR's vision is to enable people to experience personal transformation through applying God's Word to their lives and relationships.

Our Bible-based training and resources help people around the world to:
• Grow in their walk with God
• Understand and apply Scripture to their lives
• Resource themselves and their church
• Develop pastoral care and counselling skills
• Train for leadership
• Strengthen relationships, marriage and family life and much more.

Our insightful writers provide daily Bible-reading notes and other resources for all ages, and our experienced course designers and presenters have gained an international reputation for excellence and effectiveness.

CWR's Training and Conference Centres in Surrey and East Sussex, England, provide excellent facilities in idyllic settings – ideal for both learning and spiritual refreshment.

CWR Applying God's Word
to everyday life and relationships

CWR, Waverley Abbey House,
Waverley Lane, Farnham,
Surrey GU9 8EP, UK

Telephone: **+44 (0)1252 784700**
Email: **info@cwr.org.uk**
Website: **www.cwr.org.uk**

Registered Charity No. 294387
Company Registration No. 1990308